Widow to Widow:

Rawness to Hope and Healing

Widow to Widow:

Rawness to Hope and Healing

Lori Bryant-McEachern

DEDICATION

To the Great God who walks with me even in the shadow of death. John, James, Kayla, Andrew and all those who were a part of my widow walk and beyond!

PREFACE

Have you ever had to navigate a situation that came on so suddenly that your whole world turned upside down?

On October 14th, 2011, I was in that space and time where nothing made sense, and my best friend and life partner of almost 25 years was gone in a matter of hours.

Everything I had known up to that point was shattered.

I reached out to God and sobbed. I did not know what was happening. The stark reality was that I was now ripped in half from the best man I had ever known. I was now on a course that I was not equipped to handle. I stayed in shock for a long time not wanting to believe he was gone. We built a life and legacy of love that I did not think could be shaken.

He was too young to die. He had not finished raising his son with me. He had not walked his daughter down the aisle. There were still so many things to do. It now became obvious he would not see his two beloved children grow up.

The question is how does one pick up and go forward? How does a person find the strength to deal with gut-wrenching sadness, fear, and grief?

This is my story of how I went from rawness to hope and healing from the crushing blow our family took in a matter of hours. This is a story of how God orchestrated a group of providential people along the way that helped us to go through the process of grief and move forward with strength and dignity. I am compelled to share with you how one normal country family learned so many life lessons about life and inevitable death.

My story contains the devastation, numbness, and loss, untold miracles, the grace of God, and the human spirit. I will share with you some of the things that grief has taught me and the resilience and fight to live after a catastrophic event.

We will all face loss. The one thing that sticks out in my mind is that we can't cheat death, that every day is a beautiful gift, and the attitude of gratitude serves me well, even on the toughest days and nights.

These are chapters of a bigger book that changed me and the course I was on.

Walk with me and I will share a story of love, loss, rawness, and courage in the face of unbearable pain. This is a story of truth, tragedy, and triumph. I will let you into this part of my life to encourage, support, and let you know, that YOU ARE NOT ALONE!

CHAPTER 1

Anticipation!

In the Fall of 2011, our lives came to a screeching halt. I cannot remember a time I felt this kind of pain in my entire adult life. I had no idea the moments that would transpire would change our lives forever.

We were a normal, middle-class, Christian family. We worked hard, home-schooled our two children, and enjoyed our life together. We were coming up on our 25th year of marriage and planning a cruise to reward ourselves for making a relationship work for so long. Marriage is not for the faint of heart!

We were especially stressed this year and looking forward to our annual church convention. It was a special time of the year when families and friends gathered to enjoy an example of a Utopian society.

Five months earlier a Category 5 tornado ripped through our city and left a ghost town in its wake. We were all in shock! Not one of us was untouched by that horrific storm. It would go down in history as one of the most powerful tornadoes that hit the USA.

That is a book for another time.

We had been remodeling our small country home and built an addition so the kids could have their own space and we could expand out of our tiny occupancy to more space than we would know what to do with. We had been working on that project for many years. His job was sporadic in hours, and he would have weeks of downtime when he would focus on building that space. It was semi-feast or semi-famine. God always provided for our needs, and we knew it.

As we prepared for our yearly convention spirits were high as well as the excitement of spending time together and seeing old friends and making new ones. It was one of the highlights of the year!

CHAPTER 2

Excited to Get Away

We settled into our home away from home and it was one of the nicest pet-friendly condos we had ever stayed in.

Kayla brought her adored cat, Jack to accompany her. Andrew had his precious dog, Honey who he rescued when he was only seven years old. He purchased her and it was truly love at first sight.

I had recently rescued a young pup and saved its life. I called him "Pip" because he was small and full of energy!

For the next couple of days, we were together shopping, eating out, and making plans for the coming week. One memory that stands out to me is a quilt and blanket store we went to. We had been working on the addition and we were planning to move out into the new bedroom. I was looking for the perfect comforter and curtains. He wasn't showing much interest and I got a little discouraged. I said to him, "come on help me find what we want." He looked at me with a big smile and said: "I found what I wanted twenty-five years ago"! It made my heart sing!! I had been through so much with this loving man. He was seven years older and way wiser than me. I used to say. "He grew me up." I know not proper English, but it summed it up perfectly!

CHAPTER 3

911

The next morning, I noticed something peculiar about my husband. I caught a glimpse of an old man that had lost a lot of weight. This was a guy 6'1, and I was able to see his hip bones. I shrugged it off and commented that I was going to have to fatten him up! I let that go and continued to focus on our day.

The next day of our convention, he looked extremely tired and was nodding off during the services. I asked him a few times if he was okay. He would just respond that he was tired and glad we were going to get some time to relax and rest.

That evening he continued to act tired, but also said he was hungry. He fixed himself a snack. We talked and laughed! One of the last phrases he said that night was, "It's good to laugh." I have held on to that and when I get sad,

I remember there is a time to mourn and a time to laugh.

We were saying goodnight to the children and getting ready for bed when he exclaimed, he didn't feel well.

Suddenly, he grabbed the wastebasket and sat on the edge of the bed. He began vomiting I rushed to his side, and then most peculiarly he threw himself back on the bed and began thrashing about. It was one of the scariest moments of my life. He appeared to be having a seizure. Then he just stopped breathing. I prayed a guttural cry for help and beat on his chest to get his heart going again. He began to breathe but was choking on his vomit. Our daughter rushed into the room. Kayla helped me sit him up as he was choking. He fell to the floor, and she attended to him as I attempted to call 911.

This was a very unusual circumstance, and I knew we were in a Condo but did not have a physical address. The 911 operator insisted I give her an address, and I was so distraught I didn't know where to look. It felt like hours till the paramedics arrived. I was racing back and forth, checking on John and the kids, while I was trying to throw my clothes on in a disheveled manner.

We didn't try to move him from the floor. I asked where it hurt, and he said his chest and back.

Our daughter was my hero that night. She appeared to be in this tranquil place, as she sat next to her beloved Papa, wiping his face, and calming him with remarkable steadiness in her hands and her voice. She has always been so angelic, but that night topped it all. She attended to her father in the most peaceful and caring manner. I am sure her demeanor was a reassuring moment for him.

Our son was also in the room. He had just turned 13 a month before. The look in his eyes still haunts me today. He was so lost, so scared but stayed present as we tried to understand what we were observing. Not one of us knew what was happening that night. We waited and did our best until medical help arrived.

When the paramedics finally arrived, they helped lift him off the floor. The minute he stood up he began vomiting again. It was a very disturbing sight. I had never seen or smelled such pungent regurgitation. It was like he was purging a lifetime of toxins. When they were ready to transport him, the children and I followed in the car to the hospital. Before he was wheeled away, he told us all how much he loved us. His soft gentle eyes embraced mine, and I said: "see you soon." Those would be the last words we would speak.

We followed the ambulance, praying and asking God to give us the strength we would need to deal with the night to come.

Death had never entered my mind that night. I knew he was dealing with some health challenges, but I never saw this coming. In my mind, he was just too young.

We sat in the waiting room with our Pastor and his wife. I would go to the desk and ask if we could see him. She would calmly look at me and say not right now. I paced the floor and tried to find a way to get back into the room to get a glimpse of him. In my mind, we were just there temporarily and would be taking him back to the Condo that night.

The time seemed to drag on, and my patience was getting thinner and thinner. I couldn't understand why we couldn't go in and cheer him up. We were his biggest fans and supporters. He needed to see us, as much as we needed to see him. No one would give us any information that night. What seemed like a decade was finally over, we were ushered down a hallway into a waiting room.

I don't even remember how many hospital personnel were already waiting for us. The doctor was not making eye contact with me, and I began to feel my skin crawl. I impatiently burbled, "where is my husband"? She looked at me with this sad blank stare. She reported he was coherent when he was being transported, but immediately had another seizure when he reached the hospital. "Doctors worked to revive him," her voice trailed off. I was panicking at this point, and blurted out again, "where is my husband"? She would not give me a definitive answer. My mind raced to all sorts of conclusions, but nothing could prepare me for the truth!

I heard myself in an echo say, "are you saying my husband is dead"? The word reverberated like I was standing in the middle of a canyon. All I heard was dead over and over and over.

I shuttered. She grumbled, "he is for now." What? What does that mean? Is he in a coma? What was I hearing? Suddenly, I was the only one there living in slow motion, watching the reaction and movement of these strangers not making any sense.

Finally, the truth began to set in. My worst nightmare was about to be a reality! I was beyond grieved.

They took us back to show us his body. I went first, followed by the kids. It was a sight I was not prepared to gaze upon. There was my strong husband laying on a cold, hard, metal table. His eyes were still open. I reached for him, begging God to tell me they were wrong! He is going to be OK. When I touched his hand, it was stiff and cold as ice.

Immediately, I knew something had changed. I stare into his dark eyes like I had so many times before. This time nothing was staring back. It was eerie. I felt as if I was in some kind of dream, and that I would wake up and he would be there talking to me. I continued to feel his face and stroke his hair. Nothing was bringing him back. I had so many emotions going on, that I didn't know what to do. The kids wanted to see him. I know that is an image that is etched into their memory forever.

No words could comfort or console me. I was in a complete state of agony. It was as if time stood still, and I was spinning out of control. I was a wreck. I didn't know how to console my children. I didn't know anything in that space except that GOD was with us. I drew strength from the words written in the Bible about how GOD feels about the fatherless and the widow. At that moment, that is all I had.

I wanted so desperately to believe that I was going to wake up from this nightmare and have my cherished husband back. I thought, maybe, somehow, I was being tested, and that when GOD saw that I turned to HIM, He would give him back to us. He was so young, we still had so much LIFE to do together.

The tears and shrieks jolted me to reality. Our children went into shock. Not many words were spoken. They looked like they were frozen in time while I let out these blood-curdling sobs.

CHAPTER 4

The Long Night

When we went back to the Condo, each of them had their comforting pet. They cuddled them and after having something to calm them they fell asleep.

I did not sleep a wink. I called to talk to someone that I hoped would give me answers. He had none for me. He just listened to me cry as I told him how much I needed John, and that I didn't know what to do next.

The condo was quite spacious, and my uncontrollable sobs did not affect the children. I thought I was going to die that night. My chest was so heavy like someone dropped bricks on it and no matter what I did they wouldn't move. Thoughts were racing in my mind, what if I die tonight, too? Spouses die of broken hearts often. Would that be my fate, as well? The kids would truly be orphans. I prayed God would help me get through this distressing night.

When I was all alone with my thoughts and as I cried out to God, I knew it was a turning point in my life where I had to be stronger and set an example of faith. I had faith before, and I had gone through trauma, which would prepare me. I didn't realize how much I would learn and grow in my walk with God.

I was going to grow in a way that I didn't know was possible. In the exhaustion and the tears, fearing my own death that night, I determined that I was to continue to point the children to the "God who loves and protects widows and the fatherless." I was still bargaining with God and asking him to wake me up from this nightmare we were living. I wanted to go back to the hospital and tell them they made a mistake and get him out of there and take him with me where he belonged. As the night wore on, I played those events that transpired over and over in my mind.

I had to decide whether we were going to go home to an empty house or stay at the convention where friends surrounded us. We had no immediate family near us, so it made sense to stay around people. Some who had become like family.

When the children woke up, we had that discussion and we all agreed to stay until the convention was over to go home.

CHAPTER 5

Armor of God

We walked like soldiers, arm in arm in dire silence to the church building. It was like something out of a movie. Instead of being armed with guns, it was God who was giving us the strength to move.

We were greeted by stares of disbelief. It was as if we became celebrities overnight. We didn't know what to expect. We decided and went with it. The kids went off with their friends and I sat with mine.

My dear friend Becky was very pregnant with her second child. I sat with her family in the back of the building the rest of our time there.

I will never forget when they announced from the podium that a treasured husband and father died the night before. Upon hearing his name, I melted into a deep pit. It was another one of those moments where the echoes lingered in my head. I sat there trying to hold it all together. I didn't have any preconceived notions of having to be strong. I knew I was entitled to express my feelings because the 12-step program I had been in for decades taught me how to grieve.

After services people came up to me in droves offering their deep condolences. It was such a blur. I just stood there, and people hugged me, some cried, and others told their own stories. I was overwhelmed and beyond exhausted. I also felt love, and even though I was hardly able to speak, I appreciated their paramount concern and the generous compliments they bestowed upon our family.

Our children and friends walked me through the everyday motions. It was as if someone else now occupied my brain and body. I had no sense of time. I was quite oblivious to my surroundings.

My dear friend and mentor, Jill, came and stayed with me that next night. Nights were excruciating. She stroked my hair as I cried the entire night. She let me talk and cry. It was like I was stuck on a movie reel, reliving 25 years of memories. She patiently listened and allowed me every emotion I was feeling. I just wanted him back. But all the crying was not accomplishing that. I felt raw like someone had cut me open and I was trying to push all my organs back inside.

For the next few nights, someone stayed with me at the Condo. I was unable to eat or sleep much. Every day, we cleaned ourselves up and showed up for duty at the convention center while contacting and planning a memorial service for the best man I had ever known. It was surreal.

I don't remember any of the messages or how I was even able to function. It was a pure example of God doing for me what I could not do for myself. I did feel the love coming from comforting people. The kids were with their friends, as I continued to feel this abyss trying to pull me under. I lay at the feet of GOD begging to be released from the sadness that was engulfing me. I felt no good to my children at that time. I just hugged them. The only reassurance I had is that God was still on His throne. What HE was doing, I didn't know.

CHAPTER 6

Reality Hits

On the fourth day of the convention, I broke! The tears came rushing like the smashing of a dam. Dreadful sounds were pouring out of me. They were guttural sobs that came from the innermost part of my core. Reality HIT! There were people all around me as my body convulsed!! There was no consoling me on any level. I shrieked like an animal who was caught in a trap. I felt a weight on my chest that wouldn't budge. I cried and lamented until I stopped. I don't know if I stopped because I was so exhausted, or for that moment, GOD heard my cries and gave me a reprieve. The uncontrollable weeping would begin again, and I would allow myself to feel those profound, deep emotions.

My friend Mary came up to me after my public display of mourning, and said, "there is a song they are doing today, I think it will help you." I listened to the song about how we walk by faith and not by sight, and I realized I was doing just that. NOTHING made sense to me in the world. I didn't know how I would go on without him. My course was set. I would now be "walking by faith" in a way that I never knew possible. That became my motto so to speak, "Walk by Faith, Not by Sight."

In confusion and pain, I met a special widow lady at the convention. She was strong and loving and carried herself with poise and grace. We talked and she invited me out for lunch.

Claudia shared with me how she lost her husband suddenly and unexpectedly, just like me. There was an instant bond! She cried with me and gave me hope. I remember she had this loving persona and I felt safe exposing my sadness and fears. She had walked this road 7 years before me. She had 8 children, and her youngest was finishing High School when her beloved was found dead.

I shared with her that my youngest turned 13 a month before this traumatic loss of his father. I confided that I didn't know how to raise a teenage boy. Much of my fear stemmed from that. I knew in my heart he needed a father to teach him "manly" tasks.

She assured me the promises which God makes to His fatherless and widows were concrete! I held onto that like I was fighting for my life. Today, even though my children are adults now, I still call out to "ABBA, Father", who walked with us during that bleak season that seemed to have no end.

There was something so comforting knowing that others trudged a path and I was not alone. This friendship was to be one of the most enriching and special attachments I would make. Other widows revealed themselves to me and it was like I had found a new club.

People continued to line up to speak to me after services and told me how brave I was and how sorry they were about John's passing. Some were angry because they were losing a treasured friend. John had a way of making others feel special. He was a gifted listener, and his heart was made of gold. He had a deep love for others and his life showed it. He not only loved his family with passion, but he also loved those around him. His gentle kindness is something that I deeply appreciated. He would seek out the weary, sometimes tortured, and hurting souls.

He was gifted in so many ways and I was a better woman for having his love in my life for a quarter-century.

CHAPTER 7

Unbelievable Experience

I hit the fence and came to a dizzying stop. My heart felt like it was laying on the ground and I couldn't catch my breath. Did he really say that to me? I was reeling. I was dumbfounded that a man in his position would treat me with such contempt and scorn.

I stood against the fence wishing I could climb over it into some other life.

I was too tired and weak to go any further.

My pastor caught up with me and said, "We have to do this today, Lori."

You see, I had walked into a funeral home to make "arrangements" for my late husband.

I was telling the hyper funeral home director that John was taken to a particular hospital because we were at a church convention. He abruptly interrupted me and retorted, "YOU took him to THAT hospital? Don't you know they kill people there?"

I stood in shock. Questions raced through my head. What is he saying? Did I kill my husband? I felt like I was going to explode. Shame covered me like a dank, cumbersome web that I couldn't shake off.

Rage welled up inside me and I blurted out, "I can't believe what I am hearing!" Before I got the words out of my mouth, he rudely interrupted me again.

He snapped, "Get the hell out of here go somewhere else." I saw red! At that moment I felt homicidal. All I could do is run.

I still stood against the fence, recounting these events that just took place. I sunk deeper thinking this was my fault. I stood there feeling naked, raw, and brutally bruised.

My pastor ushered me into the building again, I felt helpless and hopeless. That despicable man was still there. I had no control and it felt like the warrior voice that I fought so hard for was gone in an instant.

All I could think about is that I KILLED MY HUSBAND and took my children's father from them. I wanted to die. The only thing keeping me alive was our two precious children who I knew needed me more than ever.

As we walked backed into the funeral home this director was still very agitated and began fighting again with my pastor. Round two was beginning and everything inside of me wanted to bolt again.

My pastor finally asked the man if there was anyone else we could talk to? We were ushered into a back room where a kind soft-spoken person resided. He was kind and professional. We finished our business. The rest was a blur. I don't remember anyone talking on the way back to the condo and I was beyond exhausted as we left.

CHAPTER 8

Going Home

It was time to go back home from the church convention. We did this for so many years. We always came home together. This time it was just the kids and I. Thankfully, we had friends who accompanied us, so we didn't have to face this harrowing ordeal alone.

John had stayed back to finish up work and lock up our place. Going home without him was beyond gut-wrenching.

The closer to home we got, the more my stomach ached with fear.

When we pulled into the driveway, John had wrapped a chain around our gate, like he was protecting Fort Knox! John always had a fear of people taking our things. I had to laugh! We didn't have much to take. I knew where his fear came from. His father was a survivalist and it rubbed off on him.

Once we got through the barricade, we went into the house. It was cold and one of the young men who came with us was kind enough to light the pilot to our heater.

I know the cold was not just the temperature. It was eerie being without him. There was a different aura in the house. Something was missing and I was pretty sure I knew what it was. My eyes filled with tears.

On the kitchen table was a vase I had never seen before. As I walked through the house, I noticed other items that weren't there before we left.

I chuckled through the tears! John loved Flea Markets! While he was home alone, he made a trip to the local market and bought an array of trinkets. It was a passion of his, and he filled large spaces with trinkets and some exceptionally large gadgets. I would tease him about being a hoarder. I would have loved to bicker with him about the items he got that we didn't need right at that moment. But I realized that I would never have that opportunity again.

We had a harmonious relationship amid the typical family squabbles. We did our best to respect one another and accept each other's idiosyncrasies. There were times I would get so frustrated with him when he would buy a whole box of things just for one item in the box that he was wanting. Perhaps it was because he didn't like conflict and it was much easier to get the whole box. He was a wonderful husband and father, so I chose to overlook that idiosyncrasy.

CHAPTER 9

Facing Life Without Him

As the day wore on and the sun began to set, I had to face a new reality. Nights, long arduous nights. We were at the convention without him for six days and I don't remember sleeping a wink. I was in hyper-vigilance mode and closing my eyes terrified me. I would pray and ask God for comfort for the children and me. I couldn't bear sleeping in our bedroom and the bed we shared for so many years. I took a spot on the recliner chair in the living room until my body could no longer be in that position.

The kids were quiet and seemed to be in a dream world.

Kayla our eldest was nine-teen getting ready to turn twenty in a couple of months. She had an exceptional connection with her father, who she proudly called "papa."

They were alike in temperament and personality. I loved when they would sit on the couch. He had his arm around her, and she would melt into his side, and all was safe in the world for her. She respected him and he loved her deeply.

She was turning into a beautiful young woman, and it was obvious he didn't want to lose his little girl. He was protective and involved. He was vocal about her choices and guided her with a firm loving hand.

She was a strong independent woman and continued to be a great strength to me.

The days passed in a blur, and I was having a rough time finding my footing. My world was so different now and I didn't know how or where I fit in anymore.

I knew God's promises and that John was no longer suffering; however, we were. Hours turned into minutes and the days and nights were excruciatingly long and painful.

CHAPTER 10

Memorial for John

Our next intimidating task was planning a memorial. I was in no condition to do this. I was still bargaining with God and trying to get John back.

I was still out of it. My dear friend Jill was playing interference for me. I just didn't think I could handle anything more.

John's brother and his new wife showed up and immediately began serving us. They were such a gift! Matt comforted the kids and Ruby cleaned, shopped, and made food. It was a respite we desperately needed.

I had to make plans and organize the memorial. We gathered pictures and laughed and cried remembering the fun times we had. John was such a gentleman. He was our bright spot in our crumbling fear. He knew how to make all of us feel better.

He was gone!

I wanted to ask John, "what do you want to be remembered for?"

We didn't talk about or plan for death this early in life. We were too young to plan these things. I have always wondered if one of the reasons we didn't is because it would make it too real. I wanted to believe that we would live forever, or at least he would live into his seventies.

I wanted him to see his children grow up and be a grandpa one day!

All the dreams we had made for ourselves were like an ash heap on the floor. My emotions fluctuated between rage and exhaustion.

The evening before the memorial service our refrigerator went out. I didn't think I could handle another mishap. We were tired and just wanted to go to bed. Friends had brought food that day and the refrigerator and freezer were packed.

I remember feeling attacked. I also felt despondent. I remember thinking if this is what it is going to be like without John I don't want to be here.

Rage filled every part of my body! I started throwing frozen milk jugs and screaming at the top of my lungs! The kids came out and I gave them things to throw. I told them to scream as loud as they could.

We stood under the carport throwing things at the siding and screeching in the night. We began to laugh and hugged each other. It was one of those times I felt completely powerless, but I also felt at that moment everything was going to be OK. Releasing those powerful emotions was so healing for all of us that night. I knew that if we kept those feelings locked up, they would bite us later. I saw the temporary relief in my children's eyes. This event gave us the strength to keep moving and handle the next crisis. When emotions are so on edge everything is a crisis. We took it minute by minute and sometimes second by second.

I cried all night and don't think I got much sleep at all.

It was time for the memorial, and I don't think the kids and I were ready for the day.

We were accompanied by members from both sides of the family. We did not live near any of them, so they were all coming from different states.

Music was a huge part of our life. John and I sang at our wedding reception and sang for friends and family. He was a self-taught musician and played many instruments and had a singing voice that could soothe a young baby to sleep.

It was appropriate to have lots of music and various musicians.

We picked three special people, John M., Zandra, and Mariah, to sing at the memorial, and we chose songs and performers that reflected our tastes. We also had music we performed together that had been recorded. The other performers have a special place in my heart. They each sang with much love and conviction. It was a beautiful tribute to an exceptional man.

The ladies from church had a potluck meal fit for a king. It was a special touch for all the weary travelers who came so far to honor and pay respects to this incredible man who was taken so early in his life.

There were people from all walks and times of our life who attended. A huge group of his co-workers showed up as well as the secretary and vice president of the company. It was very touching. He had been a faithful employee on and off for fifteen years.

John was easy to love. He was genuine.

I don't remember much of that day, I was still walking in a fog, but I did notice the secretary crying. She told me every day John would go into the office and ask about her ailing mother. She said she never saw him cross only kind and caring, stating she was going to miss him; we cried together.

People were generally concerned about our deceased loved one.

There was one man that came up to me and introduced himself and his lovely wife and family. Charles and Liz were some of the most beautiful people. The children were all dressed sharply and looked at me with the most angelic faces. He preceded to say that they didn't know us, but when one member suffers, we all do. I was beyond moved by this gesture of kindness. This was the beginning of a beautiful friendship. We got to know this family and for years forged a strong bond.

I will never forget the beautiful blonde-haired, blue-eyed family that made a mark on our lives forever.

People ask grieving widows and orphans: what can we do to help? They tell you if there is anything you need, let us know. I know in my case I didn't know what we needed. I was still walking in a haze for a long time to come.

This lovely family sent me cards and little soaps and self-care items. It was a treat to go to the mail and find these trinkets and the best part is knowing that she cared enough to reach out months after John's death.

We got together on many outings even though we were four and half hours away by car.

I am sad to say that 10 years later the roles have been reversed. Now it is my time to practice what she taught me.

Another dear friend of mine came and stayed with me the night after the memorial. Our friendship was strong and concrete. Pat Z. stayed in our bedroom, as I took to my ragged comfy chair. She was another friend I didn't have to put on airs. She was with me during Kayla's birth, and I was with her through her youngest son, who was born 6 months before Kayla. We both had traumatic births and offered each other much comfort and solace.

She is my "Pollyanna" girlfriend. She is the one that will always see the cup full, talk to strangers like she has known them a lifetime, and find the good in just about anyone, or anything. Her smile is a welcoming beacon in a scared and uncertain world.

She made me a beautiful prayer shawl that holds an incredibly special place in my life. We didn't get much time together because she needed to leave early the next morning. Seeing her brought comfort and her hugs sustained me for a little while longer.

CHAPTER 11

People Reaching Out

People reached out in their own way to try to console and help us. A crew of people stepped in and helped us on many fronts.

John was the breadwinner and there were so many unfinished tasks to have to deal with after his death.

One discouraging phone call that had to be made was canceling our twenty-fifth Wedding Anniversary cruise.

When the agency asked me why I had to tell him that my husband had passed away. I couldn't bear to hear those words, as I choked and sputtered. I felt gypped! I felt robbed of the opportunity to celebrate our longevity in marriage. We planned the cruise for 3 years. It was a terrible disappointment. I was beginning to feel this anger inside and the hard part was there was not a thing I could do about it. The reality was he had been taken from us and there was a strange void of darkness. I got off the phone and sobbed uncontrollably.

Our routine was shattered. The kids were trying to adjust in their own ways. The structure and discipline we had were nowhere to be found. Andrew was lost and I gave him a break from home-schooling so he could begin to process this devastation.

How does a thirteen-year-old process the loss of his father? I felt guilty because I didn't know how to help him. I was dealing with my immense grief, and he was shut down emotionally in a place I didn't know how to reach.

Kayla seemed to be doing okay from the outside. She was a leader and showed up every day to help wherever needed. She was helpful with Andrew, chores, and especially cooking. My appetite had not returned however, she was a fabulous cook and was accepted into the culinary arts program that she had set her eyes on before this unfortunate and life-changing event.

We were her willing guinea pigs, and she brought home treats that we had never seen before. I was so pleased to see her doing what she loved to do. It was a little bit of hope and healing as we tried to move forward.

I had one friend I met homeschooling. She came to visit me one day early on in my bereavement. She knew us as a couple and family for years. I admired her family and she admired ours. We had many things in common and enjoyed going to lunch from time to time.

Linda was the kind of woman who brightened up a room when she entered. Her laughter was contagious, and she always lifted my spirit. She was sensitive to others' pain, and she had never seen me in such a broken state.

Grief was taking a toll. I hadn't been sleeping or eating much. My eyes were red, swollen and tear stained. I barely had the energy to move. I lost a part of me that I couldn't have back. Deep down I was fighting for my own life and Linda could see it.

Linda was patient and kind. I felt no expectations to be all right. I sat in my old, tattered recliner, still unable to face a bedroom John and I once occupied. I remember her soothing presence and she didn't have to say a word.

I had another dear friend who had been like a big sister to me for a long time. Barb and her supportive husband, Mark, were present in our time of need.

I will never forget what she said the first time we talked. I didn't even get a chance to tell her about John's death. She heard from others.

She said, "I don't know what to say, and I will probably say the wrong thing. Teach me how to walk through this with you. I can't wait to see the phenomenal relationship you will have with God after this journey." Those were such powerful words, and I know her heart was lovingly pure. She still had her supportive husband with her and made it clear that she could not understand what I was going through..

Those were profound words and I have not forgotten them. She was one of my strongest allies going through my grief. She did not judge me and listened to my heart-broken cries. We were awfully close before this occurred; however, this cemented our friendship.

She was gentle with me and her kindness unmeasured. She had a very busy life and took the time regularly to call and check on me. She wasn't telling me about her life woes. She knew I was more fragile than a China doll and did her best to conceal her problems. This was not how our relationship was before John's death. We had a healthy share of giving and taking.

I learned how to cocoon and save my energy. I was already struggling with health challenges and knew I needed to eliminate other things that would involve much exertion.

My lovely friend Barb somehow knew this as well.

CHAPTER 12

The World Was Made for Couples

Everywhere I looked, I saw couples walking hand in hand. I would see them laughing and gazing into each other's eyes. The pain would hit me. I had trouble being happy for them. I was mad at myself that I couldn't feel any happiness when someone celebrated an Anniversary. Especially the 25th Anniversary, when we were supposed to be boarding a ship to celebrate in the Caribbean.

I felt like an alien. I didn't know who I was besides John's wife and mother to our children. That had been a huge part of my identity for decades.

I wanted to shut myself off from everyone. People we used to do "couple" things with no longer worked. I didn't know how to act anymore. I was no longer a couple, but a single woman, a widow. I could barely use that term.

This was a category of a woman I never wanted to be.

Adjusting to the fact I was no longer a couple was mind-boggling. It was one of the loneliest times of my life.

God was bringing people and activities to fill the void, but I was still feeling like a fish swimming upstream trying to re-define myself.

I let God direct this excursion of letting people into my new world. I was not able to trust my feelings, they were raw.

I was in the biggest battle of my life and leaned on God for the smallest decisions.

The gravity of losing my better half had barbs in every area of my life. We were "one" and now I didn't have him to bounce things off. I didn't have my best friend, life partner, or lover.

CHAPTER 13

Grief and The Body

I don't know if I mentioned how grief takes a toll on your health. I continued having different ailments. I started walking with the kids and found I could hardly breathe. My lungs felt like they were on fire. Each step I took was painful.

I decided to go to a massage therapist to see if she knew what was going on. She was an exceedingly kind and gentle woman and told me I had muscle knots throughout my chest and stomach. I didn't understand. I had never heard of that before. She began rubbing and releasing these "knots." I remember the first time she did I could breathe a little easier. I continued to see her, and I was feeling better each time. I noticed when I had crying bouts my sessions were worse. She explained to me that all the crying and jarring of my body caused the muscle knots. All I knew is that I was breathing better, and it was making a difference.

It is a scary place to be when you can't breathe. I've had panic attacks in my life, but they didn't compare to this feeling. A panic attack goes away after a while. This was something I was living with whether I was sitting, walking, or standing.

I spent time reading about natural health for decades. I delved into Chinese medicine and knew lung health had to do with grief. It made so much sense. I continued my treatment and noticed I could walk longer distances, until I got pneumonia.

When I was a child, I had pleurisy that weakened my lungs, and unfortunately, the grief wasn't doing anything for them either.

Thankfully, from all my health studies I knew how to take care of it. I still had a rough go of it and the kids were concerned.

I noticed it was taking a longer time to heal than it did before. My immune system was weaker, and the weight of grief made me exhausted.

During this time, I also found out my body was in adrenal fatigue. The adrenals sit on top of the kidneys and are responsible for the flight/fight system in the body. When they are not working properly it is harder to get well. No matter what I did I was exhausted.

Our eating and sleeping cycles were erratic. Grief takes a toll on every part of your existence.

CHAPTER 14

God Sends an Angel

I began to have nightmares! I observed in my fragile state something odd was happening. Growing up I was not a happy child. Certain abuses took place which I thought I had dealt with and were in the past. Suddenly I was flooded with all the deep dark memories I thought I had put it to rest. I felt weak and frail. My once safe abode became scary, and I felt like I was being dragged into a world I didn't want to revisit.

I met a widow online who introduced me to her son. He was a shut-in with a crippling autoimmune disorder and was raising a son with disabilities. The challenges with his son and his own health issues were enough for him to handle, yet he was willing to come along beside me for support.

We did not live in the same state and didn't meet face to face for a long time. We made an incredible connection and became friends. I feared him at first because of his unabashed self-disclosure. I wanted to run from him. His directness put me off. I prayed and asked God to lead and to help me figure out what I should do. God was giving me a strong message to let him in.

Skip and I talked and the more we shared the more my childhood mess came out. He told me I could call him any time day or night if I needed to talk.

We spent hours on the phone, and I cried and shared my intense emotions.

He listened and didn't judge me. He was not afraid of my consuming grief. I didn't know what my feelings were for him. I didn't know why God put us together, but I knew we were helping each other. Others judged us and misinterpreted our relationship. I was a widow. I was full of pain and there was someone who could talk to me day or night. It was a massive comfort to know there was someone available when I would wake up from nightmares or if I couldn't function because of the "day-mares."

Grief and moving forward without your companion is a frightening outlook. Knowing you have a posse of supportive friends weaving in and out of your life is priceless. I knew God brought these special friends to help me process my deep crushing despair. When God is in relationships all parties are blessed. I needed Skip during that time, and he needed me. We gave each other unconditional love and acceptance. We were allowed to say anything without fear of judgment. That in itself is a great gift. Knowing God is in our relationships provides a deep sense of comfort. Sometimes what we need isn't "packaged" the way others think it should be. I was blessed to have different ones who stood beside me and continued to share their experience, strength, and hope.

Isn't that what it's all about? Getting through this life with the help of our family and friends so we, in turn, can help others.

CHAPTER 15

Navigating the Unbearable

Becoming a widow is staggering with all the big and little changes. I thank God I didn't take John for granted. There were so many emotions running through me, at any given time and I felt every nerve ending buzzing. I feared I would blow a fuse at any moment.

I don't know if people realize how taxing loss can be. I felt crippled, sick, and lost all at the same time. I was navigating a new life and I didn't like it. I missed not talking to John about the day-to-day events. The kids were changing, and I needed help with them. I missed hearing his voice and his laughter. I longed to tell him how much I needed him and wanted him back. I cried buckets of tears.

I continued to ask for help from God. I knew he hadn't abandoned me because people were walking into our lives and giving us hope!

It was a weird feeling. On one end I felt numb and on the other end, my senses were on overload. I was aware of my fragility and iron resolve.

In my vulnerable state, there was an expectation that people would be kinder. Some were willing to meet me where I was in my grief and sorrow, and others took advantage of me.

When I told people I was a widow I thought they would be empathetic and treat me with kid gloves. Some saw an opportunity to pounce.

One situation that occurred was being stopped by a Police Officer because my license plate was expired. John took care of all these duties, which I didn't give a thought to. I cried to the Officer and asked for mercy. He gave me a warning and told me I needed to get over to the Department of Motor Vehicle. I thanked him and drove home. I went home, found the papers that I needed, and headed out to the DMV. Everyone knows the long lines and immense patience it takes to do business there. Kayla was with me, and she helped me with the task.

When we finally got to the counter the lady sitting there had the proverbial "resting bitch face." For those of you who don't know what that is, they are in a bad mood no matter what the circumstances are. I tried to explain about John's death and not knowing what to do with all the cars he left. She was smug, snippy, and rude.

I felt my temperature rise. I dared to call her out, but I just wanted out of there. We got our business done, and I walked away feeling angry and discontent. I recalled the events to Kayla, and she said, "Mama, we have so much more to deal with." My daughter's wisdom saved me again.

As I mentioned before, John had his love for flea markets, so there were many items we could sell. One time we had a man come into the house and take things, saying he would pay later, and I considered hiring him as an auctioneer. I am nobody's fool, but in my time of bereavement, I was not on my game. I was still in the murkiness of grief, and agreed, and trusted this stranger at his word. I knew my word was solid.

Days later I called him, and he refused to pay for the items. I was quite distraught and had to grapple with the idea that people will take advantage of and use me. I felt utterly defeated. I wanted to believe the world outside didn't kick their wounded when they were down. I wanted to believe I could handle my affairs as a woman and as an anguished widow doing life in a new world.

I tried to contact this man several times. It just wasn't worth the fight. I leaned on God's promises to take care of us and those who were exploiting us.

I noticed when I expelled anger, I felt extremely tired and didn't bounce back quickly as I had in the past. It was a lesson in letting God fight our battles. I never did get those items back, but I do know that GOD is not happy when someone takes advantage of his fatherless and widows. He even uses the word WOE! The Bible says He is the "defender of the widows."

I held on to these comforting Scriptures like a child with a darling stuffed animal. There's safety in these words that brought me many sighs of relief.

CHAPTER 16

"The Firsts"

I observed some people could handle the cries of the heart and others just had to walk away. I was astonished by how many walked away. Grief is such an individual process and I know for me my emotions were raw most of the time.

Walking by faith and not by sight has taught me many lessons. I had to learn to pray differently.

I realized I planned and dreamed and schemed what our life was going to be. This experience taught me to pray more fervently for God's will. I remembered my commitment to my Creator and even though I didn't understand why this was happening, I was constantly reminded that my ways were not His ways. I needed to have blind faith that things were going to work out.

Romans 8:28 was always my favorite Scripture. "ALL things work for good to those who love God and are called according to His purpose." This became a stark reality as I continued to maneuver this new "widow walk".

Ironically, I thought that I was close to God, and I was living a life of faith. However, when this happened, I could see how much I had to learn about my Creator.

He is my pilot. I am here for the ride to learn what I need to learn. My responsibility is to serve others. I have been given so much despite the trauma. We are not alone in trials. God sends a Comforter and those who have walked before us, teaching and navigating our path.

A saying I have always admired is: "When the student is ready the teacher appears." This has been true in my life. We don't ever have to walk alone. There are always others who have experienced things we go through.

It's humbling to ask for help. People in general, don't like to be vulnerable. I felt exposed and defenseless. Fiercely, I needed someone to take my hand and show me how to get to the other side.

When your whole life changes on a dime and the only hope you have can't be seen, and the future can't be accessed, this can lead to fear and despair. I needed to take one moment at a time. One day at a time was too overwhelming.

I learned there is a certain jargon used regarding a widow's experience called "The Firsts." The minute your spouse dies everything in the world changes. There is no easy way to go through this process; you must learn to live without your partner. Basically, that means everything you do after that moment is new.

One of the first thoughts for me was that I didn't know how to raise a teenage boy without his father! Andrew just turned thirteen one month prior, and John promised me he would be there. I felt abandoned by him. I went through a series of ways to blame him. I was angry that he left me with two heartbroken children and a wife who adored him.

When I would look into my children's eyes, it was as if they were not there. I felt a gnawing inside myself. Something monumental was missing. I was determined to help them despite my quivering heart.

I had learned how to do everything with John. We had been married for almost twenty-five years. Within two hours he had vanished. I could no longer talk things over with him. I no longer had the comfort of his arms around me or his smile which made everything okay.

Now there were many firsts to come.

I remember our first Thanksgiving.

The kids and I spent our first Thanksgiving with Barb and Mark. I was a wreck. I couldn't stop thinking of John and Thanksgiving pasts. We had so much love and tried to express our gratitude. That year I struggled. I remember breaking down and sobbing while Barb sat and held my hand. Mark took the kids out for a walk, so they didn't have to hear my wailing.

That was another "first" in the line of many to come.

What a blessing it was to be with someone who allowed me to be real and express my deepest emotions.

I was so grateful for the people that stayed, and the people God brought in.

My daughter's first thought was 'who is going to walk me down the aisle when the time comes'? She was nineteen and marriage was something she was looking forward to when the time was right. She lived her life and was developing her relationship with God. Her dad was a big part of her world and she cared very much about what he thought of her. It wasn't fear as much as respect. She wanted to have a marriage as we did. She wanted to please God and make the right decisions. She looked to him for guidance and direction. Their bond was unshakable.

I don't remember what Andrew's first thoughts were because he didn't share his feelings. At his age, I didn't expect much from him. I found out later that he shut down emotionally and doesn't remember much from these events. He did not know how to process this catastrophic event in his life, and I wasn't going to push him. I was worried about Andrew, tried to connect with him, so that we could work toward a semi-normal existence.

CHAPTER 17

Bitter/Sweet

Our next excursion after Kayla finished her culinary school, was heading up to Wisconsin, the place of my birth and where John and I met and were married. Matt and his wife lived there, and I had entertained the idea of moving back because we had family there.

Our current home required renovation and our beloved John was gone. John's brother and his wife came after he died to help us with some projects. We also needed a change of scenery.

We packed up our animals and headed North. We did not know what awaited us.

We were all excited to try something different.

I was hoping if the kids were close to their uncle, it would lessen the pain.

It did not turn out the way we hoped.

There were a lot of issues that transpired and for the sake of not sounding redundant, the pain again hit us like a ton of bricks.

It was not HOME. It didn't even resemble ours.

It took me a while to figure out what I was trying to do.

The resemblance John had with his brother was phenomenal! When Matt came to the memorial service, people were in awe! They commented they thought they were seeing John! I knew Matt for 25 years and we were good friends, he was a brother, and I knew he respected and loved his big brother John. It was a tremendous blow to him.

I figured out after we left their place that I was hoping the change of scenery and their papa's brother would make them feel closer to him. They said it didn't and nothing felt like home.

When we left their place, we stayed with a young family in the town where John and I were married.

We attended the little church where we exchanged vows. It was so comforting. There were even families that were at our wedding. Talk about a blast from the past. They took the kids under their wings and the kindness they showed was remarkable.

This felt more like home, and the small congregation rallied and ministered to us. The children enjoyed hearing stories about their papa. I was watching them laugh again. Several of the men showed an interest in Andrew. He learned different skills and was having fun again. He was breathing deeper, and I could see a little sense of relief.

Kayla stole everyone's heart with her sweetness. The kids knew one couple that we kept in touch with through the years. Their comfort was priceless, along with the others that reached out to show us how much they cared.

There were old friends and new ones that we met.

The young special couple, that took us into their home until we could find an apartment, was precious! We had fun with them. We laughed and cried and were so grateful to have a safe place to contemplate our next move.

I still felt very broken and exhausted. God put people in our path, always at the right time.

We met a very giving couple who showered us with food every week. I had great conversations with Steve and Laurie and realized she and I had much in common. She has been a great support to me and became one of my strongest allies who powerfully encouraged me, showering me with hope and healing.

It has been so interesting watching how God weaves the tapestry of our life. I don't believe in coincidences. I believe people are placed in your life at just the right time. Some are there for encouragement, while others are there to teach us lessons.

Relationships ebb and flow. I can see places in my life where I needed certain people to minister to me. There have been other times when I was the one serving. Sometimes we give and sometimes we take.

I think it was hardest for me to be on the receiving end. I have been a great caregiver. John and I were able to help others in various ways. It was a big part of our life together.

Grief is laborious. Everyone goes through it in their way. I learned in 12-step programs I needed to allow myself to feel the feelings that came up. I tried to be gentle and be true to myself in the process.

I mentioned that there are many people uncomfortable with deep bereavement. I loved deeply and the loss was overwhelming. I felt like I had lost a part of myself. One that I would never get back. I had to see myself through different eyes. I was no longer married. I begrudgingly claimed the title "widow." I don't like the way it sounds. I didn't want to be one. I had no control. I looked around at the couples that were unhappy and treated their spouses disrespectfully; I yearned to have my man back.

We were gold. We hadn't finished our life plans. I had to grieve what it could have been. I was powerless. I was broken. I was still alive. I didn't know where to start picking up the pieces. I felt like my heart had exploded and now I had the task of putting it back together. John was a big part of that heart that lay broken on the floor. I determined I would always carry him there as I moved forward into the new "me" I would have to become.

We stayed up in Wisconsin for a few more months. The kids and I moved into an apartment. It was very cold and living in Missouri made me realize I was no longer acclimated to arctic conditions.

I had time to think, meditate and pray. I was crying out to GOD to help me know what to do.

It dawned on me that we were paying rent when we had a house back in Missouri. We loved the old church atmosphere and the kind folks who treated us like family. I heard the message loud and clear, "It's time to go home."

It was bittersweet. We had connected with these special angels who loved us and took us out of the cold dark night. They gave us a place we felt wanted and loved. We will forever be grateful for the loving hospitality and tender affection.

CHAPTER 18

Heading Back to Missouri

The kids and I agreed it was time to go back home.

Our relationship with John's brother changed. We realized that moving up North was not meant to be. As much as we loved the idea of being closer to family and our endearing little church family, it was time to go home. I learned that when God's will is made clear, I needed to obey, and it became more evident with each passing day!

Driving home the kids and I had much to think about. When we left, we had our sights set on coming back to sell the house and moving closer to family.

I didn't want to continue living in the house that we lived in because there were too many memories. It was painful and we were in enough pain.

Andrew was happy to see his best friend! Tyler and Andrew were inseparable from their early childhood. They did everything together and had so much fun. When John died, they were teenagers. I always said that was such a difficult time to lose his father.

Andrew and Tyler grew closer and were now spending even more time together. Tyler was a compassionate and loyal friend.

Andrew continued to go through the motions as we all did. I was barely able to concentrate and so I knew his schooling was getting farther and farther behind. I enrolled him in a correspondence course to finish out his year. Kayla had graduated from the same school, and I knew the curriculum. He was a very smart child, with strong reading skills and I knew he would do fine. I was more concerned about the emotional blow of his dad's death.

We decided to start family counseling with a therapist who knew our situation. I am not sure how much we got out of it. We were still emotionally raw and struggling.

It wasn't just our mental health; it was our physical health too. Everything was off-kilter, and

I didn't know how to get back in balance. Another milestone I had to face on the widow walk was turning fifty. The kids knew this was a difficult birthday and made me the most beautiful, touching homemade cards. Kayla had been practicing scrapbooking and created a card that I hold dear to my heart. That day one of my dear friends, Sharris, brought me a sunflower mug that has become one of my favorites. We then went out to eat at a local Japanese Steakhouse and had hibachi. When the staff wished me happy birthday, I felt discouraged about being a 50-year-old widow. Tears rolled down my cheeks, while Sharris comforted me with gentleness and concern. I was so blessed to have my friend comfort me during this wave of grief. After lunch, we did some shoe shopping, which turned out to be fun and healing. It reminded me of some of John's last words, "it's good to laugh." My dreaded 50th birthday turned out to be a tremendous blessing.

CHAPTER 19

Going Back to School

I knew I had to go on, even though it felt like our hearts were still bleeding.

I decided to go back to school and pick up where I'd left off.

Before I met John, I was studying to be a counselor. I was now 28 years sober. I stopped pursuing a career to raise our family. Now my family depended on me to be the breadwinner.

It was scary and exciting to begin college. It had been 30 years since I stepped into a classroom. This is not where I thought my life was going. It was part of the adjustments that had to be made, and I had to accept that I no longer had a husband to take care of the children and me. I did the necessary paperwork and without hesitation was accepted into the program. The doors just swung open for this opportunity. I knew God was doing for me what I couldn't do for myself.

My professor in the Drug and Alcohol program was also a widow. We connected instantly, and she would become an incredibly special person in my life. In some ways, we were more like colleagues. She was gentle with me and truly understood my situation, after all, she was doing the widow walk just like me.

I tried an online class and quickly found out that was not for me.

I loved the interaction with the other students. I was old enough to be most of their mothers. I quickly adapted and began learning about a subject I knew all too well.

For much of my life, I felt like I was behind the eight ball. This time I felt powerful and engaged. I felt that deep down I was meant to work with this population because this population is ME.

I had to drive to school about 45 minutes 2-3 times a week. I often called friends on my journey.

There was one friend that I reconnected with shortly after John's death. Over the busy years, I had lost contact with her.

Ironically, we were born the same day of the same year in hospitals no more than twenty miles apart and were both named Lori!

She became a widow a few years before me. I don't remember how we reconnected. John and I sang at their wedding, and we also did some traveling together in the first few years.

She has become one of my closest friends. We have so much in common. We share a unique and special bond. We were growing and experiencing many of the life changes that happen with sudden death.

We talked regularly and supported one another in our bereavement. There is such a comfort to have someone your age living in the same circumstance. She had two children about the same age as mine that had to experience the untimely death of their father. We comforted one another and shared our hopes and fears.

When children become fatherless suddenly and unexpectedly it leaves a mark that nothing can erase.

As a wife, I had my penetrating grief and sadly I was so emotionally and physically drained I was not able to be there for the kids as I wished.

They were dealing with their sorrow.

My friendship with Lori gave me strength and encouragement. We would often talk about what worked with her children in situations and what was working with mine.

We became close quickly, and all the years that we were apart somehow vanished, and we were closer than ever. She was a powerful part of the tapestry that God was weaving.

I continued to heal, and the rawness was turning to hope and healing. God was showing me I was not alone, and that, not only was He walking with me, but He was providing a strong support system.

CHAPTER 20

Standing Up

We were beginning to heal. I sensed new energy emerging, and hope was now in my grasp.

I still struggled with health challenges. Pneumonia had claimed my lungs again. I was still healing and had to be gentle with myself.

I am always learning how important individual ways to grieve is perfectly acceptable. What works for one doesn't necessarily work for another. One thing I found that works for everybody is when people just listen.

We have such a "fix it" society and we had people in our life that wanted us to do our grieving, according to their timetable. In their eyes and opinion, we were not doing this grieving business correctly.

Words were being spewed out that we should be moving along faster than we were. I felt my safety net swaying and one could look at me sideways and I felt my skin crawl. There was a rawness of mind and body that I had never experienced.

I was angry! I was furious! I was expected to give a reason for the tears I cried and the pain I felt for a man that changed my life. I was accused of being inconsolable, and a "crying Madonna." I felt like I was having to defend my deep loss and pain.

I pulled away and stopped associating with some of the group of people who rallied in the beginning to help us. It was a new twist of fate I wasn't prepared to deal with.

I felt like an outcast. I was tired and worn out in a new and different way. I began to see people differently. My son said it best when we were talking one day: out of the mouths of babes. He said, "there are people who are great as first responders, but that may be all they can do." What a profound statement that was. They patch up the bleeding and send you to someone else who has a different skill set. I saw things in a different light after that statement he made. I realized I needed to set more boundaries to protect my fragile state.

I didn't realize some of the people that appeared cruel and walked away were scared. I was living their nightmare. I had one lady tell me this. I thought it took a lot of courage to share such a statement, it helped me see another perspective.

There was one special widow in the church to which I became very close. I always admired her and the way she carried herself. Pat B. was the epitome of classiness! She dressed snazzily and carried herself with the utmost dignity. One couldn't help seeing her poise and strength.

She walked with me and shared the lessons she learned from being a widow. She was remarkably gentle and kind, but she also possessed a firmness and determination. She was teaching me to walk the path of widowhood and that what I was feeling and experiencing others could not understand unless they had gone through it. I remember crying to her and telling her what someone would say to me and burst into tears, and she would comfort me with the same words. "Honey, they don't understand, because they haven't gone through it."

I grew to love her like a mother. I knew where to go for her understanding and tenderness.

CHAPTER 21

Enter James

I prayed and asked God to continue to heal and strengthen me. I believed it was time to focus on myself and get my schooling done so we could move forward.

A funny thing happened when I became a widow. I was getting friend requests from men I never heard of. Some were inappropriate and I had to shut them down. I felt like I was prey and being vulnerable was my "kryptonite."

I shuttered to think what a relationship would look like in the state I was in. There was also a part of me that felt if I were to have feelings for someone else it was betraying John. This was reinforced by others who were also grieving. They would say "you will never find anyone as special as John." This left me feeling sad and hopeless. I didn't want to go through the rest of my life alone. I did feel I would never find another soulmate. I grieved the idea. I threw myself into school and the kids. I prayed and continued to give my broken heart to God. I knew He still had me here for a reason and that my life was far from over even though there were times I felt my heart hurt like someone was squeezing the life out of it.

One day on social media I got a friend request. It was from a single man. My first reaction was here we go again! I didn't know him, but we had some mutual friends from our church association. I dismissed it and went about my day.

The next time I went on social media I had other requests.

I was writing blogs and articles for a worldwide magazine that our church put out. I was getting a lot of attention. People were sending out friend requests and our little family of three was becoming quite popular. The cool thing about that was my writing was making a difference for others. I was getting lots of encouragement and building bridges for others to cope with their lost loved ones.

I began to feel a sense of purpose and my writing was a great outlet for me to express my penetrating sadness, hope, and healing.

I couldn't get this one friend request out of my mind. He looked attractive in his profile picture. He had a ruggedly handsome appearance. I was wondering why he wanted to friend me. I finally got brave enough to ask. It went something like this. "Do I know you"? He wrote back. "I'm not sure, I went to college with someone with your last name."

We determined we had not met in the past and that he was thinking of someone else.

We chatted until I felt safe enough to friend him.

I was busy with school and didn't think much about this new acquaintance.

I was coming out of the fog and socializing a little more with friends.

One night I was online and so was my new friend James. I was sad and discouraged about some things going on with a group of people I trusted. I gave him a brief synopsis and he wrote something to me that magically unlocked this hidden door.

"Welcome To My World, he disclosed."

I was taken aback, and my curiosity of this man grew exponentially!

Who would have thought this simple phrase was going to change our lives forever!

CHAPTER 22

Open Door

Welcome to my world!!

It was as if someone turned a light on and I felt compelled to hear his story. We all have a life story that makes us who we are. I desperately wanted to hear his.

We had been writing on the computer for hours. He kindly asked me if he could have my phone number. I graciously consented. He called me and we talked for hours!

I went to my knees that night and prayed the same prayer I did when I met John. "God, if you're not in it, take me out." I trusted that He would guide me through this open door.

I was starting to get my feet under me and enjoying my classes. I was feeling alive again.

However, I continued to battle depression and health issues. I did notice I wasn't crying as much. Don't get me wrong, I still had many feelings and I tried to continue to address them as they surfaced.

Grief is complex. One minute I could be laughing and enjoying the moment, and then something is triggered inside, and I am hysterically crying. I learned to be gentle with myself. I learned not to judge myself and the roller-coaster I was on was where I was meant to be. I was walking through a treacherous valley I believed was going to make me stronger than ever.

I had to look at it this way so I could stay positive. God was going to give me a new pair of wings so that I could soar above all the wreckage of my broken heart.

I continued to talk to my new friend James online. We were also scheduling time to converse on the phone.

He had an incredible voice, and I learned his first job was in radio. I loved listening to him, and we would chat for hours. I discovered he was very intelligent but, more importantly, compassionate.

James' mother and one of his brothers were living with him because of illness. He took care of them and provided for many of their needs.

I was being drawn in and my curiosity began to increase the more time we spent conversing.

The kids and I were getting ready for our yearly church convention. We decided we wanted to go somewhere different. We were not wanting to go back to the site where John died a couple of years before. We wanted a different scenery. The mountains sounded like a wonderful place of peace and serenity.

One night when I was talking to James, he asked me where I was going for our convention. I told him that the kids and I were going to the mountains for a change of pace. He replied, "Me too." We began to talk about this area, and he shared he knew the surroundings well.

We started conversing in August and were going to be meeting in September.

I started to pray, realizing I was smiling more and looking forward to hearing from James. The thought of meeting him in person thrilled me and paralyzed me all at the same time.

82

I was having difficulty focusing on my studies and everything else. James would call me as soon as he got off work and we would talk on my drive all the way to school. I didn't get out until 9-10 pm his time and we would talk all the way home.

I could tell he was a protective type. This was comforting to me, and I missed the loving protection of a man. I yearned to feel that closeness again.

I was young when I married John. I was molded and shaped with him and through him. He was my beloved and the father our children. I was experiencing guilt and shame for having feelings for another man, even though I knew God was opening this door.

CHAPTER 23

Heading to the Mountains

For the past 2 years, I was undergoing another metamorphosis everything in my life changed that fateful day in October and now I was having feelings for another man. I didn't trust these emotions and didn't want to make any mistakes.

I planned to finish school and get a job in the counseling field.

I would continue to raise Andrew on my own and I knew God had a bright future for us. I prayed that if God was not in this relationship, he would take me out without hurting this kind man I was corresponding with. There was something about him that I couldn't shake.

I was still looking forward to meeting James.

The time came to head to the mountains for our annual convention. It used to be the highlight of the year, but not since John died. The memories were still fresh and raw, and we still walked around like zombies at certain times. The kids helped load the van and we were on our way.

We caravan-ed with other family and friends. I didn't get much sleep before the trip and honestly dreaded going. I was nervous about missing so much school. I tried to get my assignments done, but I knew I was going to miss class time.

I communicated and stayed in touch with James on and off the whole trip. I was exhausted and still dealing with my adrenal fatigue. We also were having trouble with the van. He told me not to worry about it and he would look at it when we got there. His words felt comforting in his protective way.

Kayla and I took turns driving. She loved to drive, and I didn't. Andy was in charge of keeping us awake.

When we finally arrived, and I saw James waiting for us I felt like crying. He was there to help us unload and get settled in our cabin.

I got out of the van and threw my arms around him. It was like I knew him, and our souls were suddenly united.

I introduced him to the kids and after unloading the van he took us all out for dinner. We didn't talk much, and the kids were checking out this new stranger who popped into our lives unexpectedly. They were not sure what was going on and the rawness of losing their dad was especially hurtful this time of year.

After dinner, he drove us back to our cabin and we said goodnight. I was feeling an array of emotions and wanted to stay grounded in the moment.

I spent time in prayer and drifted off to sleep in my temporary home. The lavish accommodations gave me peace. I intended to fully enjoy it!

CHAPTER 24

Shame and Rejection

Two years ago, my husband died at a similar convention. I would be facing people who knew me as "John's wife." I had such mixed feelings. I wasn't feeling well, and my body felt worn out from the trip. I still showed up! I went through the motions of getting dressed and fixing my hair. The kids were getting ready, and we drove quietly across town.

I was still reeling. Just being at this convention flooded my mind with memories and terror.

James was spending the day with his family elsewhere. I didn't expect to see him at all. He was still very much in my thoughts.

There was a definite physical attraction between the two of us. I felt a little awkward and it was obvious that he did as well. He didn't make any time for dating while he was taking care of his ailing family members. He put his heart and soul into his work. I admired his dedication to his family.

That evening was tough. I was reminiscing about two years ago when I lost my true love. What was I doing with another man? I was in so much pain over John's passing and still was. I wanted to run away. I felt guilty about feeling alive again. I was thinking about how nice it felt when James and I hugged. I yearned for physical contact. I struggled with my emotions and kept pushing those guilt feelings away.

After all, I wasn't doing anything wrong. I was a widow and free to re-marry. There was this conflict going on inside me, so I took it straight to God. I believed He was leading James and me. I just didn't know if I was ready.

A message came through from James as I was grappling with my conflicted feelings. He was telling me he didn't think things were going to work between us. In my tender state and the riotous emotions, I just sobbed. Was I ready to be with someone else when my heart was still broken from John's passing?

I stayed awake much of the evening crying and praying and that turned into the next day. I tried to hide my tumultuous condition from the children. They left and went to meet up with their friends. I stayed back and felt my deep feelings of rejection.

I told myself I am not cut out for dating. After all, it had been over 27 years. I didn't know what I was doing. I felt awkward and it felt like I was betraying John. I wasn't ready to give my heart-broken pieces to another man.

The part I struggled to understand was what am I doing here? James and I connected on the phone and had this incredible bond. We were both praying and asking for guidance and direction. This felt like a sucker punch to the gut. I wept hysterically! I fluctuated between tears and anger. Why is this happening to me during the toughest time of the year? I sobbed and felt inconsolable. I felt foolishness for believing God was bringing us together. I was still such a mess.

CHAPTER 25

Twists and Turns

One thing happening to me in widowhood that cast a shadow on everything was the fact that my body felt like it had been through a wringer! I had lost weight in my grief yet that didn't make me feel better. I had constant aches and pains. Not to mention the pneumonia that plagued me. I was in a fragile state.

I determined I would go back home to finish my schooling and get a counseling job. I would put this all behind me and focus on raising my sweet boy who had been cheated out of a father.

There were these gnawing thoughts in the back of my mind. What happened that made him send that message to me? I told God I wasn't going to ever see him. Part of me couldn't believe what was happening. I was prepared to accept God's will and move on.

I don't know exactly how it happened, but I was to hear from James again. I was cold and had my boundaries sky high. He told me he had an emergency at work and needed to head home. Good, I thought. It will make it easier to not have to see him. I bravely confronted him and asked why he would send me a message like that?

He replied that he was trying to process his feelings and had written several things never intending to send anything. He said there was a conflict going on with his family and the internet at his cabin was acting up. He asked for another chance and said he really needed to see me.

I was still furious! I was deeply hurt. Did I want to give this man another chance? NO! My heart was already broken and fragile. I didn't need this.

He told me he would call when he got back and would like to take me out on a real date. I said I would think about it. I was not making any promises.

I was being stubborn! I was guarding my heart-broken fragility and was in no way letting my guard down. I had been traumatized and in my delicate condition didn't need any more heartache.

I had the next couple of days to think about it and my resolve didn't change.

One evening the kids and I were at a restaurant with friends. There was a long wait to get a table for such a large group. I was outside because large crowds and noise caused me to feel panicky. Someone opened the door, and I heard a distinctive voice. It was James!

I was still angry, and he told me he wouldn't be back for a few days yet there he was. I felt betrayed! I decided to call him and see what he would tell me. I was hoping to catch him in a lie. I know that sounds terrible but, I was not going to let my guard down one iota or let him off the hook.

CHAPTER 26

The Call

I dialed his number, and we were in such close proximity I could hear him on the phone and in person. He proceeded to tell me he took care of his business at home and got back early and was meeting his family for dinner. I felt a smidgen better. He asked where I was and told him outside of the same restaurant waiting for a table. He came outside and talked to me and wanted to introduce me to the part of his family that was in the restaurant. He asked me if he could escort me to the table with the group I came with. My reply was cool, and I said, "If you want." I was not budging, and my emotional walls were still high, and I was trying to assess if he was just a player.

We went in to be seated and many of the people next to me were ordering drinks. The wine was whispering and enticing me to partake.

James was sitting next to me I told him I had to get out of there. He knew I didn't imbibe and that I was recovering. It had been decades since my last drink, and I wasn't going to be around it.

We graciously excused ourselves.

We went to a different restaurant, and I was quiet and didn't know what to say. I was still nurturing my wounded pride. I didn't really know this man and was not going to let him hurt me again. I continued to pray and ask God to help me maneuver these treacherous waters. I felt physically safe with him and knew he wasn't going to hurt me; this was a matter of the heart. My heart was still fragile and guarded. I felt I needed to be vigilant, so I didn't feel misled.

I don't remember exactly how our conversation went that night, but we decided to give it another try. James explained to me that he had never dealt with such strong feelings in his life. We had been talking and getting to know one another for over a month. We both had unique circumstances and being cautious was part of us.

He came from a broken home and at his age never dreamed anyone could make him feel the way I did.

We continued our heart-felt disconcerted conversation. He shared that he didn't think any kind of relationship was going to happen for him. He worked hard and took care of his ailing mother and brother. I could see the compassion and tenderness in his eyes and yearned to be an understanding friend. I could feel my heart melting as he recounted his fear and trust issues. We were connecting on a whole new level.

When he dropped me off, we set a date for a motorcycle ride in the mountains.

I was excited and scared, but I was walking by faith and not by sight, knowing that God was holding my hand.

CHAPTER 27

The Big Ride

This was one of James' biggest passions. He had been talking about his love for riding motorcycles shortly after we met. I was never on a bike, but I was willing to give it a try.

I will never forget the feeling of freedom I had that day! It was chilly up in the mountains; nonetheless, the exhilarating ride launched me into another dimension. Breathing a sigh of relief, I began to relax for the first time since our misunderstanding.

I didn't want to stop riding because I was encountering a spiritual experience. I felt a closeness to God like never before. The sun was brilliant in the sky and the penetrating rays warmed me. The mountain was so close I felt a part of it.

James told me that he had been interested in motorcycles since he was 5 years old. He informed me that was how he relived stress. He continued to say; each time he went for a long ride he came back centered and focused. He joked with me and asked if I had ever seen a motorcycle at a psychiatrist's office! He said when you have a motorcycle it's not necessary. We just laughed.

It was his outlet to put things into perspective. I believed him! I could honestly say I had not felt such euphoria in a long time. I was sold! I wanted to ride all day!

We pulled up to a restaurant and as we were walking in, James looked at me seriously and said, "You know if the roles were reversed, I would have gotten my face slapped." While we were riding, I was holding on to his chest! I'd never been on a bike before and wasn't sure how to hang on. Apparently, my hands were a bit too high. I turned a bright red and they showed us to our table.

Talk about breaking the proverbial ice. James informed me that he was voted 'Most likely to say anything' in high school. We talked and laughed the rest of the day! I have never lived that down. James likes to tell this story to people we meet, and we laugh!

We had a wonderful first date and all the misunderstandings seemed to fade. We drove back to his place and continued talking until evening. We met the kids for dinner.

I was equally impressed with how he handled the children. The kids were struggling and not ready for me to have a gentleman caller. He managed to get them laughing by watching Christian comedy. James and I were laughing, and I saw the kids above us in the loft peering over listening to the show. We invited them to join us, so they came down and sat in the room and we began enjoying ourselves. The pressure lifted and then James invited us all to dinner. I was impressed by the way he was able to soften them.

One more issue that needed to be addressed was the mini- van. Among other skills that James had, he is a mechanic. He came over and fixed my van so the kids and I would be safe driving home.

I felt secure and protected with him and going home meant we were not going to see each other. He lived in the east, and we lived in the mid-west. I was constantly praying for God's will. There was a lot at stake, and I vowed to raise my teenage boy and finish school so I would be the career woman I thought I was being led to be. Somehow this changed something.

When it was time to leave the convention and go back to our perspective homes we promised to stay in touch. It was an invigorating moment, and our last date was heading into the mountains to go stargazing. I knew this was the start of something wonderful.

CHAPTER 28

Returning Home

The kids and I got back into our routines, and I felt lighter. I dared to dream that I would find someone to who I could relate on such a passionate level. James and I had so much in common. It became increasingly difficult to focus on my present life. I wanted to experience more of him.

We talked whenever we could. We both had a thirst for conversation and getting to know each other better. It was becoming obvious to us that we were made for each other.

I realized that I was changing. I was not the same woman I had been a few years earlier.

I had metamorphosed into a quieter, somber, and somewhat melancholy woman. I had become more seasoned. The gregarious and bold personality I once possessed became lost in an ocean of heartsickness. I was entering a phase of my life that I had imagined was going to look diametrically opposite. I knew I couldn't change the past and needed to move forward to see what God was preparing for me.

Nevertheless, something inside of me was waking up! Even though I was feeling this major shift inside me I dared to dream. I was optimistically guarded. I knew I was in a vulnerable position, and I did not want to lean on my own understanding. At this point in the process, I had developed an incredible dependence on God.

Some naysayers cautioned me on getting involved with anyone. Others were outraged and indignant to see I was already considering a new relationship. I learned how to set firm boundaries.

From a young girl, I was a warrior in spirit. I had to overcome obstacles which gave me a gift of discernment. This gift grew exponentially during this grief-stricken phase of my life.

Walking by faith possessed a new meaning for me. Trusting a process in which I was not privy to the outcome had its terrifying moments. I had to walk away from relationships and silence the voices of others so I could hear God.

I learned how to get quiet and listen for that small inner voice where my God resides. This type of meditation was new to me. I was on the go for much of my lifetime. I was learning a deeper, profound, and confident way to live.

I was discovering this new freedom to be me. School was showing me my life was far from over. I realized under the shroud of grief there was some spunk left in me and a raging purpose to thrive.

It became exceedingly laborious being apart from James. It had been a month since I had seen him, and it felt like years even though we talked most evenings. Nonetheless, I had responsibilities and needed to focus my attention on the kids and school. School was taking on a new meaning for me and I didn't want to be distracted. After all, I was getting my training because I had to take on the role of breadwinner, or did I?

One day while we were talking on the phone James mentioned he wanted to fly me out to see him. He exclaimed that he missed me and thought with my small break from college coming up now would be a great time. It didn't take him long to convince me because being apart was taking its toll on both of us.

The children knew that I was very interested, but I could see their pain when I talked about him. They loved their papa and were now wondering who this mysterious intruder was and what his intentions were with their mama.

I was praying and seeking God's guidance the entire time. I didn't want to make a mistake and those around me slung unsolicited advice including being too soon and waiting until Andy is out of the house. "You need to heal more; it takes 10 years to recover from a loss such as this. You don't want to marry a selfish bachelor. There is a reason why he hasn't been married before now." On and on this kind of advice was being thrown at me like spaghetti on a kitchen cabinet door. It was a good thing I had my armor on to withstand these barbs of criticism.

Nonetheless, I was growing closer in my walk with God and did not intend to let others sway me from the steps He was leading me in.

CHAPTER 29

Flying Out East for a Visit

Suddenly I was on my way to the East coast and the anticipation was immeasurable!

My heart was bursting with joy and apprehension all at the same time as I boarded the plane. A thousand thoughts raced endlessly in my mind. James and I had been talking every day and spending a sizable amount of time on the weekends conversing.

I sat on the plane reminiscing about our time in the mountains. I thought about the breathtaking motorcycle ride. Feeling the chilly brisk wind as we rode up and down the mountain was exhilarating! My heart was smiling, and I dared to dream about the new life which was unfolding in front of me. My mind stayed steady and listened for God's continual guidance. I was aware of my vulnerability and wanted to make sure James and I were on the same page.

I saw that James was a valiant God-fearing man. He impressed me on so many levels. When we were with the kids in the mountains, he took opportunities to include them. There were genuine attempts to show them a nice time. He would perpetuate a light-warmhearted atmosphere that included humor and laughter then he would round everyone up and we would do something together.

I was jarred back to reality when the flight attendant asked me if I would like something to drink? I politely asked her for some water. As she walked up the aisle, my mind began drifting back to the first time I met James.

Abruptly my mind shot to a place where I felt fearful and ashamed. Did I have the right to feel happiness or was I supposed to stay a grieving widow? Instantly, I felt confused and wondered if it was too soon to be dating. I spent 25 years out of a lifetime with John. Did I know myself enough to be exploring a new relationship? These thoughts thrashed back and forth in my mind-boggling state. I wanted to get off the plane. I silently cried out to God and once again uttered the prayer I used decades ago. "God if you are not in this relationship, take me out!" An immediate calm fell over me and I felt a supernatural relief.

I was exhausted! I was still dealing with a host of grief-stricken health challenges.

However, the anticipation of getting closer and closer to seeing James began taking the highest precedence. I felt like a giddy schoolgirl ready to start swooning for a boy crush! I was not going to visit a boy nor was I a young girl. I was a 50-year-old widow being thrust into a new universe.

People continued their unsolicited opinions about my life. It was aggravating to hear others so compelled to tell me how to live my life. As this process continued my walls grew higher. This wasn't bad. I was developing a deeper union with my personal God, as well as the counsel of my friends.

James was an inspiration. He was taking care of his mother and disabled brother for years. His father left when he was eight years old. Yet his tenacious spirit forged a life of consistent service to others. I saw a fighter with a heart for God. I wanted him as a friend and more. My feelings were unshakable, yet I knew I needed to stay level-headed.

The pilot announced we had reached our destination. I felt butterflies in my tummy, and I found myself taking deep breaths!

Exiting the plane my legs felt like jelly. I wondered how I should greet him.

James was not an overly affectionate man. He lived with four brothers and physical touch was not a huge part of his life. On the other hand, I love to hug. I am warm and affectionate.

He was there waiting for me by the baggage claim. I smiled and gave him a quick hug. He was all about getting my luggage and getting out of the airport. I wanted to savor the moment. He seemed to be in a hurry much of the time. He was energetic and moved at a swift pace.

He lugged my suitcase in his car, and we were down the road when I realized I would be spending a long weekend with his mother and brother who lived with him.

I was excited to spend time building a bond, yet I was keenly aware of her dependency on

James and there could be potential issues. I was determined to put my best foot forward.

When we arrived, we spent a little time settling in. His mother was affable, and his brother was quiet.

James had to go back to work for a few hours, so I was alone with his mother. We chatted superficially as the clock ticked. I couldn't wait to be reunited with James. There was an ease I felt around him like I knew him my whole life.

Finally, James walked in the door and my heart jumped. It was raining so we had to forgo the motorcycle ride. I was disappointed although I didn't dwell on it because we were going to be spending the rest of the afternoon and evening together.

We were getting to know each other on a deeper level. We were discovering how remarkably compatible we were. We loved the same music and grew up in the same era. Our views about life fit like a glove. When he held me, it was electrifying yet I felt safe and protected. He was a man's man, and I could feel myself falling faster. I wasn't sure if the attraction was more physical or spiritual. I felt this astounding connection and he confided in me what he was feeling.

"Whoa, slow down girl," I told myself. We were friends and yet the more we shared the bond was feeling eternal.

We had a fabulous time together and saying goodbye was sad. I was so emotional I cried, and he gently comforted me, which made it even more difficult for me to leave. I could feel my heart healing and the pain that covered it was slowly melting. God was leading us into new territory, and we were both in for the ride of our lives.

CHAPTER 30

Recovering Energy and Hope

Back home, I had work to do. Deadlines for school projects were looming. My kids didn't know what was happening and I tried to explain. They were not ready for big changes. In some ways, they were stuck and didn't know how to get past their dear Father's death.

I stayed busy and tried to spend quality time with the kids. We would have random chats followed by tears. We were all determined to heal and move forward. We knew that was our only option.

The kids could see they were getting their mama back. My schooling was going fabulous, and my new romance had me in a state of joyfulness. It was a big change from all the crying I did. Bit by bit my heart was healing, and my energy was improving. That made the kids content and more settled.

Kayla was looking at continuing her plans for school in Texas. She made a list when she was a teenager and had a specific plan for her life. Of course, losing her "Papa" was never part of the plan, but she knew she still had her life to live. She was working in her culinary art field but wanted more. It was good to see her getting focused and making plans.

Andrew was getting back to his studies and still spending lots of time with his best friend Tyler. I loved their friendship and how they would create games and have fun exploring out in the woods. It was good to see him recapturing his childhood and being lighthearted.

CHAPTER 31

Thanksgiving With Friends

James decided to fly out for Thanksgiving. It had been a month since my visit. We planned to share a meal with two of my closest friends Mark and Barb. We decided to pack as much into his visit as possible. Mark was a pastor, so we were going to do some relationship counseling. Earlier we took a compatibility test for couples and were anxious to see our results.

I spoke about my friend Barb earlier. She was the one that asked me to teach her how to help me in my time of bereavement. We also spent our first Thanksgiving with this extraordinary couple. The kids loved Mark and Barb. They were like family, and they stood by us through thick and thin.

We picked James up at the airport and suddenly we were in a warm embrace. My heart was beating as I felt his strong arms around me. I felt safe as we stood there hugging.

We drove back to the house chatting and talking about the excitement of our long holiday weekend.

The kids were a little quiet until they warmed up a bit to James. I could tell he was tired after the flight and needed some rest, however, he informed me that he did not nap during the day. We just chatted and enjoyed each other's company. We were used to talking every day, but it was wonderful feeling him next to me.

We were making plans for our guests to join us for Thanksgiving. Kayla and I prepared a gluten-free meal because of our sweet Barb. It was a challenge for Kayla and me; however, one of my favorite things to do is spend time with my kids. Kayla's experience with cooking school and her talent helped her embrace a new undertaking. We spent the morning in the kitchen while James and Andrew set up a new computer James designed for him.

Everything turned out perfect!

After dinner, the kids went outside, and we conversed with our friends. This was the first time they were meeting James.

We sent the results of our compatibility tests separately to Mark. We were about to hear our results. Mark was sitting comfortably in the recliner looking mischievously upbeat. Mark was easygoing and had a gentleness that always put me at ease. He was closer than a brother!

Mark began, "I have been doing this testing for many years. Rarely have I seen anyone more compatible than you two."

We understood that he worked with more young people than older ones like us.

I felt a sigh of relief as James squeezed my hand. Mark went on to say that he did not see any issues that the two of us could not overcome.

We spent the rest of the afternoon chatting and sharing stories of our lives.

I was still fighting pneumonia and breathing was a chore especially when there were bursts of laughter! We were having a wonderful time bonding.

It came time to say goodbye to our dear friends! When they left James and I went and relaxed on the couch. The kids were in their bedrooms and James said he had something for me.

CHAPTER 32

Evening Surprise

He proceeded, "I am not good with words, and you know how I feel about you." He handed me a small box and asked me to open it.

Inside was an exquisite shining sapphire ring. It was absolutely breathtaking! I was ecstatic! I hugged him and expressed my undying love for him. He told me he had never felt this way about anyone and wanted to marry me.

I was overjoyed and a resounding YES emerged from my lips!

It was a whirlwind weekend, and my heart was full! I knew this would be difficult for the kids. After James left, I sat them down and told them James and I were planning to be married. I explained we had no details worked out. They knew it was coming although didn't expect it this soon. I told them we would work things out and talked to them about our plans. They were both quiet and didn't say much.

Our relationship was moving at a rapid speed. I knew that I was insistently requesting God's perfect will to be revealed. There was no doubt James caught my eye and was continuing to impress me daily. My thoughts fluctuated between deep love and admiration for James to a pang of foreboding guilt for John.

I spent over two decades with John, and we had an extraordinary relationship that was reinforced and nurtured. The children recalled that they were grateful for our blessed stable home life. John and I both grew up in families with oodles of fighting. We determined we wouldn't live in a toxic environment. We invested quality time in us and the kids. It was excruciating to see them hurting and questioning their future, but God was showing me a new path and I knew He wanted me to embrace it.

John and I briefly talked about the forbidden topic, "If something ever happens to me, I want you to remarry." A subject no one wants to dwell on. Yet, I lived that nightmare and I know it had a powerful effect on the kids. They were still healing, and I was introducing them to a brand-new man that we were going to be living with. It was a grueling concept for them to swallow. I wanted the transition to be as painless as possible. James and I would seek God's perfect timing!

CHAPTER 33

"Unlovable"

The cynics showed up again and this time with a vengeance. A woman I had known for years found out about our engagement and was exceedingly cruel. Her words pierced me like a sharp knife impaling me to my core.

John had a way with people. He never thought he was better and treated each one with dignity and respect. Many of the "unlovable" found a place in his heart. People that others dismissed he took the time to listen and comfort. One of the people that told me early on that I would never find another Christian man like John shouted, "John is rolling around in his grave. How could you do this to him!?" Her words rang out and seemed to scorch my heart.

I was already dealing with my own fears and unnecessary guilt. I was so vulnerable and even though I had my spiritual armor firmly intact those fiery darts managed to penetrate and wound me. I chose to discontinue contact with her. I needed to be supported more than any other time. I would choose to forgo ridicule or judgment.

I have learned through this process and "let go" of people who conducted themselves in an unfit manner. My energy was minimal, and I needed all the energy I could muster to get through the coming months.

My mind had to make a shift. When I proudly wore my two-carat sapphire engagement ring I received peculiar and gawking stares. People would ask me what the ring meant. I reasoned because it wasn't a diamond others felt compelled to ask. Some believed it to be a friendship ring because they thought it was too soon for me to even be considering a new relationship.

With this, all said, what I believe to be true is that everyone deals with grief in their own way. All these people questioning my judgment knew John and loved him. The feelings of betrayal I was experiencing compounded my immense guilt. I was angry and wished people would leave me alone to run my life. I continued to seek God in this enormous mental and emotional process.

James was comforting and continued to point out that I wasn't doing anything wrong. We were both absolutely convicted God brought us together. It was starting to feel like a Romeo and Juliet scenario. We refused to let the drama change us.

James was level-headed throughout this entire process. He supported me and listened to my tearful mournfulness. It was painful to have people give such harsh judgment. I couldn't deny what God was doing despite the wrangling.

Life went on and I needed to focus on schooling before winter break. I had several projects and tests to take. The kids were doing their thing and we were all copacetic. They were still numb and didn't say much about the news. I knew this was a delicate situation that needed to be handled with kid gloves. We were all in a different stage of grieving, and this new development was a challenge to endure.

On the other hand, I was beaming with excitement. I couldn't stop thinking about what was happening to me. I wanted to believe I could find love again. However, I didn't think it would be this soon. I certainly didn't believe it could be so perfect and magical.

A lesson I have learned is when God is in the center everyone is blessed. I find that comforting and a reason I tenaciously seek God's will.

CHAPTER 34

Spending Time with My "Fiancé"

Before I knew it, I was flying back out to be with my 'fiancé.' I was now in my fifties, and it seemed odd being a bride again. This trip was about finding a home for the six of us. Yes, I said six. James's mother and brother had been living with him for some time. I knew they were part of our packaged deal.

Spending a full month with James and his family was eye-opening. I realized his mother was extremely dependent on him and this would be a tricky transition.

I was gullible and believed his mother would be so elated for her son she would give us her blessing and we would live happily ever after riding a motorcycle into the sunset.

On the contrary, she was suspicious, and hateful at times, and I could see that her claws were just below the surface. James had to work, so I was left at home with her. It was quite intimidating, and I felt incredibly uncomfortable, and we had many silent awkward moments. It seemed like hours before James would come home for lunch. We would steal a few moments away only to have quizzical eyes following us. I felt trapped! I wanted to impress his mother and show her how much I loved her son. It just wasn't working. Even though she had other sons James was currently helping her with her living expenses. She raised five boys on her own and had a stubborn pride that couldn't be denied.

Even so, I tried to find a place in her good graces. After all, she would be my mother-in-law. I wanted a smooth transition, especially for the kids.

James and I agreed to marry in our hometown and then the kids and I would move to his corner of the world. It would be a monumental undertaking, but the kids reluctantly agreed.

I was starkly aware the kids and I were moving away from everything and everybody we knew! I was exceedingly concerned about their well-being and how this significant event would affect them. They both struggled with depression and deep sadness. Grief counseling didn't help much because they were in such a robotic state. When the inevitable can't be denied there really isn't much one can do.

We were getting along in the best way we could. I prayed diligently for them and believed God would see us through.

It was an extremely fact-finding trip and James and I had tons to discuss. We were merging three families and it was not going to be idyllic. I was immensely protective of the kids, especially Andrew who was now an older teenager. James and I had many talks about how to handle this shaky passage.

After a couple of weeks with his mother, I began to feel terrified. I tirelessly tried to find common denominators.

I was beginning to see this was not a battle I was going to win. I wanted her acceptance, but she had a peculiar way of engaging me. I felt like a fish on a hook and when she reeled me in her words were disturbingly painful. She appeared conniving and spiteful. I felt like I was walking in a mine field and never knew when I would set her off.

After a couple weeks I felt like I was living the definition of insanity: doing the same thing over and over and expecting different results. I was exhausted. I expressed my feelings of defeat to James. I felt like I was failing him because I could not connect with his mother.

James was tender-loving and incredibly sweet. He knew I needed to get out of the house. However, it had been raining for days, so we took the jeep. As we pulled up to the Bass Pro Shop, I felt a release and began crying. He knew about my waves of grief, and he graciously allowed me to break down in front of him. He didn't say a word, he just held me. Truly there was nothing that could be said at that time to console me.

CHAPTER 35

Hunting for a Home

One main reason James flew me out was to search for a new home. The place we were going to be living together. I had to keep my focus on this joyous occasion and not allow his mother to come between us or dampen my spirits. This was challenging. While James was at work, I had to find other things to do. I stayed in his room and exercised, read books, and only made an appearance when need be. I took the opportunity to walk outside when it wasn't raining.

James' brother Kevin, who lived a few states away, was in real estate and he helped us find our home. It was an incredible deal, and we were so grateful. I knew the kids were used to living in the country and that was our biggest priority. We would not survive in the city. Kevin set us up beautifully. The place was perfect for us. It was a spacious 4 bedroom, 2 bath on 2 acres of land. It's dominantly wooded in a private picturesque setting. It was all that I dreamed of and more. There's a section on the property I named the "Alcove." It is perfectly nestled in between a canopy of trees. I found myself saying, "Thank you, God! Thank you, James, and thank you, Kevin!

Before I had to go back, we needed to secure the loan. James and I were sitting in the bank and the loan officer informed us that the computers were down. We needed to make this transaction before I boarded that plane. Time was not on our side and if the computer didn't work, we would lose the house.

We believed we were following God's lead in our unification. I wondered if I'd missed something. Had I missed a clue that we were not to get this home or even marry? I prayed silently in that moment, "If you are not for this relationship take me out! If you are and this deal goes through, I will love James with all my heart for all the days you give to us."

The loan officer walked back into the room sat at her computer and tried again. This time everything went without a hitch. We were buying a cozy home in the country. I was marrying a man God handpicked for me. The proposal was stupendous! My heart was so full of gratitude and peace.

I had a plane to catch, and I had lots of things to do to get ready for this monumental move.

CHAPTER 36

Reuniting with my Children

Immediately when I got back, I kissed the kids and showed them pictures of our new home. I could see this was a bittersweet proposition. I slowly introduced more information about our upcoming move.

This was going to be an unbelievable task to complete. John and I accumulated tons of personal possessions and objects we would not be lugging across the country. The difficult part would be how to distinguish precious memories and let go of things that no longer would serve our needs.

I felt a tremendous amount of stress trying to decide what to keep and what to put in the auction. I felt completely overwhelmed with the chore that had to be done. It was a walk down memory lane which was not something I wanted to do. I was still distressed from the traumatic events which happened just a short while ago.

I still dealt with guilt and felt an uncanny amount of shame. When you are married for the length of time, we were it's not easy to switch gears. With that said my heart was opening again and I was not going to pass up this opportunity to experience another loving marriage.

We had many misfortunes and dishonest people that surfaced. It was disheartening to have individuals lie and steal items right in front of us. I felt vulnerability take hold of me and I couldn't shake it. I wanted to be strong and firm, but my resolve was weakened in this unfamiliar process.

The kids were given the task to go through their belongings and sift out what they wanted to keep and what they were willing to part with. It was an intimidating opposition and Andrew had an exceptionally hard go of it.

In many instances, it felt like I was frozen in time. Everything inside stopped and I was unaware of the present world. I watched my kids experience this process. There were times they looked like deer in the headlights. It was as if we left our bodies and were just going through the motions.

One minute we were laughing and the next minute one would leave the room. It was disconcerting on every front. We gave each other the space to grieve in our own way.

I honestly don't have clear memories of that stage of our recovery.

I knew on some level the kids were wanting to get away from our current lifestyle. It was a heavy demand to pack up all our belongings and move out of state. The kids were willing and crept along at a turtle's pace to evaluate their possessions.

CHAPTER 37

Preparing for the Big Move

School was exhausting and dealing with adrenal fatigue was not helping my cause. As scatterbrained as I felt I had no option except continue my current path. I loved the interaction of my schooling. As time progressed, I became more distracted. I had all these looming projects, and none could be ignored.

James was working and in his spare time zealously preparing our new home. We decided to get married after I finished school in May. There were countless chores which needed to be done before we could pack up our memories and say goodbye to those who had enriched our lives for the past several years.

I opted not to be there for the auction.

James and I communicated as much as we could despite our busy schedules. Once the auction was over, I would be able to breathe a sigh of relief. We knew we had to let go to embrace the new life awaiting us.

Some people voiced their opinions regarding how quickly James, and I were engaged. Let me tell you something I learned looking back on this transformation. I was utterly broken. Our lives were tattered in a million pieces. I knew God in his mercy could only be so kind as to open my heart and bring someone who he prepared for me and me for him. All along we both sought God's guidance and loving friends who had our best interests at heart.

We were not young teenagers just acting out on a whim. We were two middle-aged adults who had a strong connection to God and a fortified support system to lean on.

We knew the kids were struggling but were willing to move.

I thought long and hard about our decision to trek across the country and uproot the kids.

I knew it would be hardest on Andrew. There were times I wanted to back out. I planned to continue my college program, and get a good job, then when Andrew was an adult, we would get married.

We were on a path and God was directing this time frame, not me.

The auction day arrived, and I was sticking with my plan not to be available. At the last minute, the auctioneer informed me that I needed to make an appearance.

I don't even want to talk about the auction. It was more agonizing than I ever could have imagined. I had to show up because they were also trying to sell the house and property. Looking back, it was not a good move on my part. Much money was burned up in the advertising. It was a fatal flaw in my plan.

It was difficult seeing our belongings go for pennies on the dollar.

God was showing me a bigger picture and that was to continue trusting him.

The house did not sell, so we had to deal with that for months to come.

Many families moved out of the area after the category five tornado that ravished our town just about a year ago. This changed the housing market and it affected us.

Once that part of the journey was complete, I could focus on the wedding which was getting closer and closer. James and I hadn't seen one another since January.

I finished my classes early, and they had a little goodbye send-off. I earned a 4.0 GPA for the entire year of school. It was exhilarating. I hadn't been in school for close to 30 years!! I felt new confidence which I carried with me. The hard work paid off and my re-entrance to college was a major success.

CHAPTER 38

Wedding Day

The kids were packing up the things they intended to take with them. The wedding was scheduled, and we decided to make it very small. James had to be back to work shortly after and we planned on having a honeymoon in the mountains on Memorial Weekend. Excitement was in the air and a new life awaited us.

My dear sweet friend Debbie made my bouquet and all the other decorations. The colors we chose were royal blue and bright yellow. It was stunning.

Pat B., my widow friend who became like a mother, was to be our witness and the one to sign our marriage license. After John died, I found myself running my decisions by her. She was exceedingly supportive and encouraged me in a manner that allowed me to find my balance.

I remember her wise words to me, "They don't understand honey, they haven't been through it." Somehow this absolved the ludicrous things people would say and do.

I was extremely proud and chose her to be the one to witness and sign our marriage license. She was there with me during my numbing pain and now shared a part in our immense joy.

We were bustling around getting last-minute details into place for the wedding. We had a small group attending for various reasons. Time was of the essence, and we were leaving town in a couple of days.

Everything fell into place. We were married in a quaint lovely courtyard. I remember the sun was shining and not too warm on this glorious May afternoon. I felt happy and hopeful about our new life. James was a man of God and his actions toward me were true and honorable. I was proud to become his wife and to share this unknown journey together.

Many thoughts were racing through my mind in those hours. I still had an ache in my heart and could see the children were struggling with this event. They were quiet and cooperative, yet I knew they were embarking on an unknown journey.

Kayla and Andrew looked marvelous. They were willing to work together for my happiness and joy. My kids have never been great with change and this move was colossal.

When the moment arrived to walk down the short corridor to my new husband I was wrought with anticipation. There was this gallant giant of a man who was never married willing to take my children and me into his life. This spoke volumes to me and his commitment to our love and happiness.

When I was walking down the aisle the sky hues and brilliant sun enveloped me. When I looked to my right there stood a tall dark chivalrous man. He was dressed in a white suit and a royal blue t-shirt. My heart thumped! A smile came across his face, and I felt my grin match his. From the moment we met, I knew God was doing something special. It was as though we were handpicked for the other. There was a familiar comfort we both felt and were determined to nurture its growth.

We stood gazing at each other while the sun beamed brightly illuminating the start of our new life together. I felt blessed beyond measure and a feeling of peace that surpasses all understanding filled me with delight.

We all took a leap of faith that day and had an exciting new course ahead of us.

EPILOGUE

When I think about the long journey this has been, one thing I am absolutely certain of is that God held my hand and brought other hands to guide me through the devastating grief and pain which felt paralyzing.

Bit by bit, each moment spent in the tears and the fears of monumental changes we were not alone.

This book was written to give a voice to grief and let every widow know, <u>"You are not Alone."</u>

In an ocean of desperation and fear when the memories and triggers knocked me out of balance, I found GOD holding me and bringing me to a deeper awareness of how powerless I was, but also how loved. I could not control what was happening. We were not going to get our treasured family member back.

I stood in that "shadow of death" and learned how fragile I was and that in that fragility, I became stronger than I imagined.

I faced demons that I never thought would be in my world. I learned about people, the goodness and the wounded who taught me lessons about who they were and most importantly who I was and the gifts I had been given in the face of tragedy!

I saw a side of my children which was both gut-wrenching and inspiring. Watching them grow into adults and taking this experience with them. Losing a parent isn't just a one-time event, it is a lifetime of the moments, the big ones and the small ones which shape our lives.

I found the statement, "He's in a better place," redundant and annoying at times. He may be in a better place, but we weren't. We too, were fighting for our life and forging new and unfamiliar roads.

We were the casualties of a broken world where death exists, and heartache is an ever-present stigma.

We walked hand in hand in a marriage that was sanctified by God and then in a matter of hours he was gone.

Grief is an individual process, and no two people experience it alike. We are all unique and so is this transformation that never ends. It changes and morphs us into different beings. I think that is one of the things that makes us human, living in an ever-changing world.

I have felt the gamut of emotions which brought me to my knees. Walking by faith and not sight took on a total new meaning as I groped in what felt like a dark, dank basement, where I learned how to safely close my eyes and trust a God who promised to never leave or forsake me. I realized I can be in a place of utter desperation and unyielding agony only to look up and see a sign from heaven that everything was going to be okay.

I have always been aware of my surroundings. Experiencing the loss of my husband put me in a whole different level of awareness. I was seeing and feeling things that captivated me and sent me into unfamiliar terrain.

I spent time going through the stages of grief in my deep desperation of crying out to God to change it. I bargained and begged for God to bring him back. I cried, I prayed, I felt these immense feelings of sadness and I didn't know what to do with them.

In my mind I knew all my efforts to change the outcome were futile. It didn't stop me from trying.

I felt these changes happening inside of me and barely had the energy to speak. I went from weakness and barely wanting to live to fighting with my whole being for my children. These were dark and foreboding days, weeks, and months. I didn't know how to go on or even if I wanted to.

I struggled with a heaviness in my heart that I thought would never go away.

"Look for the good in each day" one of my mentors counseled me. I practiced that and wrote in a gratitude journal. There were still things to be grateful for even though my heart was crushed and broken. In this stage of the recovery process, I was desperate for any glimmer of hope.

I was desperate for any feeling of relief and movement to a different state which I found myself in.

I read somewhere that no significant changes should be made in the first year after the death of a spouse. I understand that now more than ever.

The vulnerability in that first year was staggering. I tried to keep the kids on some sort of schedule, and I failed. Kayla made a huge change in the first few months and went to Culinary School, which her heart was set on. It was the right move for her advancing her dreams. Andrew and I got lots of tasty treats that we had never had before, so we appreciated her labor of love.

I am not one that believes we should "should" on people. I make decisions based on several factors. I was keenly aware that my decisions needed to be deliberate and carefully and prayerfully processed.

You have heard me refer to my process as the "widow walk." It was a time in my life where I gained so much wisdom and grace. I cried out and told God what I needed. I forgot at times that he was directing this excursion and I needed to trust what he was doing. At times, my faith wavered. I didn't think I could make it through life without John and especially when I looked at our two beautiful children and their broken spirit.

It drew us closer together in a long run, but I made many amends for not being there for them in my overwhelming spastic existence. It was like being in a constant state of premenstrual syndrome (PMS).

When I went back to college after so many years, I found a new excitement and purpose. I knew I was the breadwinner now and needed to figure out how to step into that new role. Counseling was the only thing I knew and could do well. It was an obvious choice, and I was ready and willing to throw myself into it.

It was such a positive experience and gave me a new strength and confidence.

I learned that it was okay to give myself time to repair and then time to rebuild. I trusted God and his guidance as I listened intently for that "still small voice" that was leading me along this barren pathway. I was like a child seeking direction and guidance and ready to DO the next right thing.

My "mama bear" was awaken deeper and I became mom in the classroom. This was a role that I felt extremely comfortable with unlike "widow." It was a title of a group I didn't sign up for and was still having a difficult time accepting. I would remind myself, "Acceptance is the answer to all my problems today." My thinking and my attitude were a challenge to keep in check. Being in school gave me a new purpose and place to serve others.

You have heard the song where it says, "you can't hurry love," well I found you can't hurry grief. Things change in this life all the time. None of us are exempt from loss and we must do our best to navigate and learn to accept the unchangeable. The serenity prayer reminds me of this.

"Lord, grant me the serenity to accept the things I cannot change.
courage to change the things I can
and the wisdom to know the difference."

These are deep concepts and what they taught me is that the only thing I can truly change is myself. Learning to be proactive and not view myself as a victim I found that I can be victimized without carrying the extra burden of owning "I am a victim." There is a big difference. Having other widows in my life and hearing their stories taught me I am not the only one who has gone through this unpredictable "widow walk" and frankly more women join the ranks every day.

I feel my responsibility to share what I have learned and pass it on. My hope is that it will bless your life and give you strength, courage, and the will to share with family and friends. Give yourself permission to be gentle with yourself. Give yourself time to heal and determine how to walk in a forever fluctuating world without your partner. Learn to listen to yourself and trust something greater than you

to take you through the valley of the shadow of death.

Remember the blessings each day holds and find the gratitude in each moment. I feel I live a deeper fuller life knowing how quickly it all can vanish.

I still experience fear and have to combat those feelings with prayer and meditation having my journal close by to jot down something inside that needs to come out.

I don't make apologies for the cries of the heart. Those triggers can come from nowhere and knock me down. I now accept those as part of the process. I am reminded when you love someone deeply you will grieve deeply for them.

Then my heart opened again when the right person for me came along. I thought my heart would never heal, slowly and suddenly there I was being introduced to another loving man. It was a struggle and emotions ran high. Trusting God and knowing how he was changing me in those two and a half years to unite in marriage again was not what I expected.

I looked at life in a different way. I became less black and white. I learned to embrace the new me and allowed myself to love and support another man. I was wiser for having experienced the loss and yearned to love this way again.

I went from rawness to hope and healing and made space in my heart to love deeply and completely.

Twenty-five years in a loving marriage taught me so many lessons. Marriage is a beautiful union I was ready for, by the grace of God, and all those who walked with me and walked beside me until I had the strength to stand on my two feet.

What a story God is writing, and I am excited to see what the future holds.

Made in United States
Troutdale, OR
07/21/2023

11464312R00090